Perfect Mess

Rebecca Phythian

Bent Key Publishing

First published in Great Britain by Bent Key Publishing, 2023
Copyright © Rebecca Phythian, 2023
The moral right of the author has been asserted.

ISBN: 978-1-91-532023-0

Bent Key Publishing
Office 2, Unit 5 Palatine Industrial Estate
Causeway Avenue
Warrington WA4 6QQ
bentkeypublishing.co.uk

Edited by Rebecca Kenny @ Bent Key
Cover art © Samantha Sanderson-Marshall @ SMASH Design and Illustration
smashdesigns.co.uk

Printed in the UK by Mixam UK Ltd.

For Mum and Adam.

Contents

Perfect Mess

Toast, Part 1

A smaller me,
Plaited hair and rounded glasses
Sits, subdued
Feet just surpass the edge of the couch

She has a temperature,
Poorly —
Not quite well enough for school

Mum buzzes busily in the kitchen
Because this wasn't often the case;
Her daughter in a midday embrace
Because her face is burning up
But she isn't panicked.
She has the perfect remedy:
Toast.

Warburton's white,
Each piece cut up into four small squares
Times two
(That's eight)
Surrounding the plate of beans
And the glistening gold of margarine

She brings in the plate
And the state of tiny Rebecca's face
Changes.
Rearranges into a half smile
(The first time in a while)
And as she sits with her toast and beans
Watching Top Cat on the TV
She feels whole, and for just a few mouthfuls:
Better.

I Am a Perfect Mess

Game Face

This is my game face
In the rat race
We call society

Words with strong sentiments
Slip from my lips
Relentlessly
Because they matter

As do the poets beside me.

I carry on so that I can pass the
                              baton
                                    To the next
To inspire
And see what may transpire
When belief is instilled

And you have not only filled your own cup
but someone else's

That is my game face;
For many more than just me.

Roses

The sound is intense.
Music drums and hums beneath the floorboards;
I am surrounded by a cacophony of voices
And to me it could easily be
100
But it's not
I know it's not —
So I try not to make a fuss.
Instead
I smile, gaze around, hope to cross paths
With another person's eyes
Connect
And pretend
To be fine.

We move and order food.
The crowd grows,
The music somehow shooting through my mind
Like sparked impulses, a million neurons.
My blue-cheese fries arrive
And to my surprise, they have a sauce
Dripping over them so spicy that my head swells.
My head swells
I don't feel well
In fact, everything has become so much for me to bear
That I can't help but stare at the glare of arcade game screens.

I eat and pant like a dog.
Hot in the heat of summer,
I'm uncomfortable
And everything seems to be smothering my senses
In a way I can't understand.

I excuse myself and leave.
Swiftly.

I drift through Manchester city streets;
I sob and cry and try to fathom why this is happening;
Why I feel like a complete and utter failure
For feeling,
For being —

I am worn down by all that consumes me,
All that I keep close to my chest —

And as I ponder these weighted thoughts,
Picking up fragments of my abyss
I turn a corner, and

The most beautiful, pure, golden light
Pours into Piccadilly Gardens.

I stop.

I'm just going to take a picture of the sky, I won't be a sec.

Snap

A moment captured

Sorry, I hope I've not put a dampener on your day.
I think I just really needed to talk to someone.

It's okay.

I buy myself roses.

The ones I saw the other day but didn't buy
Because I thought they were too expensive.
They were reduced
And I took that as a sign that could help define the rest of my day.

And in a way,

They did.

Later

A soft breeze passes my cheek.
I see plants; branches and leaves sway;
The water is calmer than before
And everything feels easy. Tranquil.

In a few hours from now
I will have forgotten how this feels
So let me revel in it a little longer.
I feel stronger like this.

I Am Not a D*sney Princess

I wouldn't say I was a Disney princess;
I'm just too much of a perfect mess!
I'm more like Snow White's mate, Dopey:
A purple hat but I won't bat
My eyelids at the guys.
Instead, I'll win the prize of their friendship.

You won't find me in a gown and pearls
Like Cinderella and the girls.
I don't care if a prince thinks I look pretty;
I'd rather someone think me witty
But that kind of set-up is not my style;
I think I'd rather wait a while.

Now. Princess Aurora, I hardly adore her:
A prick on the finger, guaranteed a stinger,
It'll only linger for a minute, so just get over it — Jesus!

I couldn't be a mermaid;
I'm not the best when I swim.
Although, I would look for any excuse to
Serenade my *Him* —

Belle goes through Hell
With a hairy beast put under a spell.
Above and beyond?
An unbreakable bond...
Or just completely ridiculous?!
And I am **more** than suspicious of the talking clock.
To mock me would be
Offering a ride on a carpet that's magic.
What kind of tragic chat up line is that?
No signs of commitment and we're already in a spat.

Race and religion, I'm completely open to:
It shouldn't stop someone from falling in love with you,
But Pocahontas. Mate.
You're in a state over a guy you've known for days...
I spy with my little eye — *a phase.*

To Mulan, I can relate —
Though she has far too much on her plate:
Fighting for China, what she believes is right,
Selfless acts in circumstances that *might*
Change the world...

From hereon in is where I begin
to see my traits in the fates of Disney girls...
But there is still too much fantasy to be real.
For a quirky, strong, witty, anxiety-ridden Mancunian —
That doesn't appeal.

Tiana has an inner fire, which I really admire
But don't workworkwork until you retire!
Live and breathe your own lifestyle...
Even if that means less money for a while.

Rapunzel yearns for a life outside of her tower
And later realises it is *she* who has the power
To sing in the Snuggly Duckling — even if it's seedy!
And that wanting compassion doesn't make you needy:
It makes you human.

Merida makes a stand
By winning her own hand
She is incredibly brave
But maybe her fave...

Is a girl.
Maybe she wants to give that a whirl?

The Princess-to-be
Makes friends with Te Fiti:
Defies expectations from her relations.
Being courageous is not outrageous;
She has the balls
To stand tall
In the face of danger, and
Rather than being a stranger,
She becomes a hero.

My future has not been foretold.

Who knows whether it's a glory to behold,
But I know I will live it freely
And make mistakes on the way:
For life isn't always breezy,
So I'll take it day by day,

Let my soul connect
With a love that will protect the dreams
That seem to ooze from my pores
because I want more from this life.

I want to see sights from the heights.
Bask in the glow of my equals
And together we'll make sequels
Because the prequel is too good
To stay stuck in the mud;
Waiting, hoping, dreaming of
What could be.

That's not me.
I'll make great things happen myself
And leave my own story on the bookshelf.

So, no.

I wouldn't say I was a Disney Princess —
Because it'd be too perfect to say yes.

Empty

Let me lift the weight from your shoulders
And kiss your forehead tenderly

You mean everything
Though I am empty.

Root Rot

i.

Time elapses.

My stem
Turns from light to dark

My flower,
The thing that somewhat defines me
Is wilting.
No longer bright,
Light,
Almost fluorescent in its glow —

Leaves become limp.
They no longer have strength within them to grow.

I have adapted to my surroundings before:
I have thrived
I have grown
I have moved in ways that surprised even me
But this —
This is root rot.

My core is crumbling
In plain sight.

There seems to be
No second chance for this weeping willow
I won't have you at aloe;
No longer succulent with flair,
I feel Yucca.
Inch by inch.

I wouldn't feel you pinch my leaves back even if you tried
So leave me in the compost pile
And say your last goodbye.
There's nothing left.

ii.

She's never been one for giving up
And when she loses touch with herself
She'll often turn to nature
To find solace

And in this compost pile
After a good night's sleep and an ounce of hindsight
She sees a window of opportunity
Ready to cease —

For this plant wasn't in as bad of a state as it seemed.
There's a single, small stem trying to branch out
With beautiful, healthy leaves
It's simply been overshadowed by darkness and doubt

So she takes the plant
And holds it with care
To remove the limp leaves
Here and there
Whilst getting rid of the old soil
(Along with any unwanted thoughts.)

She takes a pair of scissors and cuts an inch or so
Under the brand-new, sprouting growth
And it hurts
Even though she knows the rest of the plant is dead.

Maybe neglected, discoloured and unfed
It still felt hard to let go of.

She plans to propagate and wait,
Leave in water to hydrate
And then when long roots are formed and ready
She'll repot.

New life.
New home

It'll thrive
On its own,
This little cutting

And that's enough for her.
She needs no more or less
Because she found light in the darkness,
Gave herself another chance
And at a glance,

I think she'll grow just fine.

*

I don't know feeling,

loving, or healing either.

Numb: wholeheartedly.

She Is a Perfect Mess

Nurture

Nurture her
She needs it
More than you can see

It is hard for her to exist
Peacefully

She wants
        Calm
In the palm
Of her hand

But it turns to quicksand
Before she can understand it
Or fully grasp the feeling.

Healing is hard.

Toast, Part 2

Throughout her teens and early twenties
Rebecca learned how she liked her liquor and booze:
She would dance, sing and let her aura ooze from her pores
As she let go of weighted thoughts and tension
With totally wild abandon

But

You'd think she'd have learnt
In that time
That white wine was not her friend,
That too many gins
Would pin her to the floor
Shivering
Tingling
Feeling the furthest from herself as she tried to stay awake.

Shall I make you some toast? Mum would say.
Rebecca would nod.
She'd been sick more times than she could count

But Mum never said a word.
Never scorched her with shame
Or put the blame on to her —
She was young once, too, and probably did the same
(If not worse, knowing Mum.)

Sit here, eat that and watch the film.
Disney's Aladdin played...
Dizzy Disney's Aladdin played
While Rebecca tried to stay upright on the couch
And crunched on carbs sporadically,
Feet on the floor this time.

Mum went to bed
Her heavy-footed stomps loud on the stairs
A bit worse for wear

As they'd been out together
And she, too, was frazzled.

Venom

An instinct
A sea of red
Fury
Shades over her eyes
Fills her veins —
She is threatened
She must defend
She spits venom
With all that her tortured mind has to give
Blind to those who feel the burn
Blind to the erosion of her own skin
Nobody wins this round
Nobody asked her to fight
She stands alone in the ring
Tired
Weak

She can't pretend
That she doesn't take everything
To heart
That her eyes don't smart
From the aftermath of tears
For fear she has hurt someone dear
Everything she wants
Feels out of reach
And no matter how well you teach her
This will happen
Time and time again

*

She picks up the remnants of her shattered heart
Sc a t t e   re d on the ground around her
And she begins to fix herself
Piece by piece,
Because she now understands what she deserves
And that was something
Greater
Than what you gave her

Listen

Listen.
Silent whispers rest on her lips;
You can only hear them sometimes,
So pay attention.

Deep red
Unread lines
Etched into her skin,
Written in invisible ink;
Not visible to the naked eye
But very much present
(To her at least)
Do you believe her?

I hope so. I'm ashamed to say.
I'm ashamed to say, but I hope so —

If you look the other way,
You might lose her.
If you stand too close,
She'll shiver at the shock of heat on her skin.
You can't win,
But she can't either.

She wants you to stay
But feels far away
From everything,
Everyone —
They can't hear
Her raging loud
Quiet.

She's clutching at straws, really;
Trying to keep the peace,
Maintain the feeling of anything that rises to the surface
But
Nothing comes.

All she can do is exist
And try to move through it.

And all you can do
Is listen.

A New Chapter

From the depths of pain, despair and uncertainty:
She steps forth.

The people that had faith in her all along are smiling widely.

Her mind swirls with possibility, excitement;
She's trying not to be scared, but she's anxious... very anxious.
It was to be expected,
When it never truly goes away.
But this was the change she needed —
Craved —
And so she can't help but stand a little taller,
Bravely anticipating the good to come.

Ready.

Take up space, my dear

Your space

You need not fear your potential
Or the torrential torment that falls heavily on your mind.

It may take a while to find your courage,
To step forth;
You might have to fight a little,
Relight the candle wick;
That flame that once burnt bright within you,
And let them hear you.

But trust me when I say that it will cause no outrage,
Like the kind you've imagined in your mind's eye —

Those around you;
Watch how quickly they surround you
With admiration and awe.
They *want* you to succeed;
They will not put up their fists
To resist what you bring to the table,
What you stand for —

Stand.
Proud.
Let the sound of your voice ripple through
The pool of people that want to listen

They have always wanted to listen

In fact, they've always wanted to take up their space too

And maybe the reason for them doing that
Will be

You.

Love Is a Perfect Mess

I Don't Know You

Meet me in the forest
And let our first date
Be foraging for berries.

Let us dance and sway
By the river's edge
From the break of the day
Until the setting sun sits peacefully on the   edge
Of the earth.

Let us feel the chill of night
And let it remind us that we are alive
And oh, how alive we are —

We will lie under moonshine and shooting stars
Tearing the sky apart
In the most extraordinary way we've ever seen.

And I tell you about my dreams,
What I think they mean

And of the something I've seen in your eyes
That somehow feels like home.

Did I meet you in another life?

Layers of Intimacy

Our first meeting:
A smile, a greeting
A gesture of kindness
Proceeding to coffee, chats and endless quizzing
To fill in the missing answers
Gaps in my knowledge of the person who caught my attention
All those months ago.
Let's go —
Drinks, shots, dancing, flow
Our bodies meet in the heat of this club
Our silhouettes suit
But mute any further feeling:
He's a brother from another mother

Call him:
Heartbreak,
Consoling;
They were so controlling
If only I could have the qualities of my best friend
In a boyfriend
I think, but don't speak it aloud
But I'd be a liar if I said I hadn't contemplated
Debated what it would be like
To date him
Kiss him
Maybe even... fuck him.

Nope.
It won't transpire.
Instead, continue as normal
Happy and content
Quality time spent

Watching Treasure Planet together
For the 100th time

How much of it are we spending
As friends
When in the back of our minds
There is a seed of intrigue
Growing gradually into something bigger?

Level up:
Physical touch
More hugs, cuddles, exchanged glances
What are the chances of this happening?
You and me?
Because I see your eyes change when you look my way,
Breathing in this familiarity
Standing on a firm foundation of trust we built together
Whether something more ever happens or not
I love you, a lot.

The laughter;
Rapture upon rapture of joy
Intense and pure.
But it had to change, couldn't last the way it did.
Our meetings became infrequent
Conversations decent
But shorter.
I miss
Him.

Never have I ever been this honest with anyone.
Never have I ever loved someone like him.

Platonically, at least.
The tonic to my gin.

Wine,
Dine,
Dinner and a show
At the theatre with a guy;
Nice, fine...
But he's flirting and I'm tipsy
I don't want him on my lips, see
So honesty is the best policy
But honestly
I just want to see *him*.
The best friend, the one working across the road
If I call now, I might strike gold
And be able to see him.

Ring ring
                    Hello?

Win. I'm in.

The station is quiet and he enters through the arches
My heart is pounding with a tipsy tingle
But as I pull back from the hug he holds me in
I notice a spark I haven't felt before.

Years in the making:
I'm his for the taking.
In that moment, I know we will never be the same again
And I fret time and again over losing him as a friend
But surrender I must, to the depth of feeling I have for him.

He
Is beautiful.
So close to being mine,
And as I lie with him, our limbs intertwined,
My head on his chest,
I see the rest of my life
Flash before my eyes

With him in it.

My love.
My best friend.

The person to whom I am connected
By intricate intimacies,
Layer
    upon
        layer of connection

Verbal
Physical
And some that lie beyond our comprehension
And always will.

Still... I wonder what layer of intimacy we will uncover next?

You Tapped My Glasses

You tapped my glasses and I landed in a new dimension.
This new but familiar feeling is like a dream that I'm in.
Pinch me!
Do you feel this?
Oh, tell me that it's not just me.
Tell me you see two stars in alignment
In orbit of something greater than what we ever knew;
Something I'm scared of, but still want;
Something I can't deny no matter how hard I try and believe me,
I've tried
And failed, happily.

Echoes of MJ's *Baby Be Mine* rush through the air
And it's fair to say my smile is the biggest it's been all year.
Who needs fear?
When I've got you here, I don't fear anything.
And I'm standing on the brink of a beautiful existence with you,
Wondering whether to jump

But I think I already have.

There Is a Place Like Home

Soft curves of burning amber
Rest effortlessly
Upon grey clouds

In another direction
Is a pink, coral-like shade
Helping the sky drift
From day
To night

White lines
Pierce through the light blue
Constant
And I'm reminded of you

I feel like I'm coming home.

There's no place like home
Except, there is a place *like* home
That feels more homely than lonely
And it isn't here

And I'm reminded of you

It's about time the winds changed
It's about time I embraced it
Because it's getting harder for me to face it

It is humming in the background of everything I do
Humming in the background of everything I do

Nothing new
Questionable living

Not thriving
Just feeling
Everything
And some things that shouldn't be mine to feel

There is a place like home
And it's somewhere I know I'll belong
With you.

Cactus

I could be as prickly as a cactus
And you'd still hold me
Caress my spikes selflessly
And while I speak and move defensively
I know, deep down, that you're
The greatest comfort I've ever known.

You teach me to not give in to the spikes
Of frustration, torment and despair;
You help me to accept that they are there
But not to wear myself down by worrying they'll consume me
Because that's consuming in itself.

Infinitely

I feel for you infinitely.
So when I say *I love you*
My words will never summarise the capacity
Of feelings I have for you.
Look deeply into my eyes
And see the stars, the moon; galaxies in their infinity
Feel the warm glow that radiates from me when I'm around you
Let it sink into your skin.
Let this connection between our two worlds
Allow us to orbit one another
Creating a singular entity
An energy.
Strong, blazing with light: beautiful.

I don't know if soulmates exist
But these feelings persist
And my connection to you
Is so fierce and complete
That I can't ignore how I want you —
Need you —
And that feeling of being whole when I'm with you?
It makes me a better version of myself.

So when I cry as we have a deep meaningful conversation
About how we feel
And we speak so honestly and freely about our raw and real
Feelings about each other, it's not because I'm sad:
It's because my capacity for love has grown into something
Beyond my comprehension and I'm learning where to store it
And how to show it to you in any way I can.

Hold my hand and I'll hold yours.
Kiss me and I'll kiss back.
Tell me you love me and I'll look into your eyes with intent
So I can tell you without words
How I feel for you so infinitely.

Him

The softest of touches
The strongest of love
Effortless affection...

I miss it.

Awe

I am awe
Struck
Whenever I look
Into your eyes.

The shimmer of hope
Sparkling
In the emerald, earthy, ever
Green

Grounded
By the roots you have grown,
The flourishing buds of passion
You've shown

They shoot from every limb
Every pore
And the more
I look and see
The more I want to be
With you.

I am awe
Struck
When you hold
Me
Intimately
Kiss me tenderly

And I,
Sheepishly shy,
Close my eyes.
Hide away:

Close to your chest
To rest
my weary head
In the safest space
I've ever known.

I know
Why I
am awestruck.

Because loving you
Is unprecedented to me

It is as easy as taking a breath:

Limitless.
Free.

Doughnuts

Kindness
Is what oozes from your pores
Like sweet, sweet jam from a doughnut
And the first taste of sugar on my lips was so full of wonder,
That before I knew it, I'd eaten a five-pack
And fallen for you
Deeply.

You were confident and self-assured
Yet sensitive.
I'd soothe
                A beautiful soul
                    Like yours
Any day.

Spectrums of colour would bubble under your surface
And I was the only one that could see you
For who you truly were:
Magnificent in your entirety.

End game:
You.
The two
Of us:

I got to call you and tell you I loved you
I got to kiss you and nuzzle into your neck!
I got to walk and talk with you,
Hand in hand,
As we effortlessly faced life together.

Whether the sun shone or not,
There's not a lot of people who can say that

In the way that I
        Can
          Could
            I can
              Can't I?

Forgive me, sweet kindness;

I'm struggling to remember,
To recollect my thoughts and memories:
Everything is
Laboured,
Harder
Than before

The soft touch of your lips against mine
Or the safety I'd feel as our limbs intertwined
It feels like a different time
Drinking wine whilst fine dining
Eyelids batting
Butterflies wings flutter
In tummies
Full of Piccolino's pizza...

But now I'm stranded on an island
Of not knowing where to go.
I lie here wondering why
Searching for answers like long-forgotten footprints in the sand.

You were everything I needed
Encompassed into one human being
Glowing beautifully

Like the sun on a winter's day
And I loved you
In the way I always had and even more:

More —
More time —
I'm waiting by the sea
Wondering if you'll follow me.
Where do I begin?
How do I let you in?
Lost in my mind...

Will you throw me a lifeline?

Find
Me
Again.

Embrace

You embrace me
And whatever is
Or may be
Is put aside
For a few moments

I am reminded
Of warmth
From another
And the comfort I find within it
Within you

The two of us
Held
Whole
Complete

In the heat of this
Embrace.

Maybe we aren't ever going to reach 'happily ever after'

Maybe stories are just stories
Fairy tales are just pipe dreams
And we are just meant to see
Where life takes us.

Maybe gasping for breath at the surface of the water
And trying to catch the rubber ring
You've thrown into the stormy haze
Is the easy part.

Maybe being torn apart by waves
More often than you care to say
And letting them tend your wounds
As you roar like a beast who's wounded
Is the closest thing to togetherness we'll ever feel.
I'm trying to heal.

Peel away the layers of dead skin;
The voices that lie within
Twist and turn their daggers with vicious words
Until the heat and defeat simmers on my skin:
Burns, scolds, scorches
And I retreat

I retreat often.

*

Like a creature entering the world after hibernation
I take baby steps and breathe in the air I forgot was there,
Forgot I needed:

I am tired, weak and hungry for something

I'm hungry for stability:

For three meals a day,
For a daily walk away from the city,
For less time on screens,
For more time showing you I care.

My candle was burning at both ends
And I was burnt out so quickly
That everything became a fight;
Either that, or I tried to take flight.
I couldn't be talked out of it
My mind played tricks,
Mimicked the Devil
And I revelled in dark thoughts of loneliness and hate.
Let me dissipate when no-one is looking...
Let me.

The realms of darkness we sometimes feel
And conceal so as not to scare others
Are scary in themselves:

I'm just lucky that I know when my mind lies
And when it's time to speak
And we will continue to reach peaks of despair and want to tear
Our worlds apart because we don't deem them worthy
But no-one wants that
No-one ever said they wanted that
So don't do it
Don't do it

Don't give in.

You're not weak for feeling
You're freaking out and it's fine
Your mind needs time to come around
To the sound of other voices
And kinder choices
And not the ones you hear in your head.

Rest now.
Go to bed.

Sleep.
Dream.
I'll see you in the morning
And you'll feel better.

I promise.

We Are All a Perfect Mess

*

Hold out your hand, my love.
Let me give you my heart
And know that until we part,
You are its keeper.

Somewhere We Can Rest

I dream of the day
We can sit
Lie
Side by side
In a way
That releases the tension
We hold onto
From the modern world

I dream of the day
We can lie under the stars
with our hearts
As full
And calm
As the steady sea
Just be
Together

I dream of the day
We'll float
Upward
Momentarily suspended

From earth
No gravity
Just us
And the crescent moon.

Note to Self:

Today's worries and tomorrow's troubles
Will feel insignificant
When you're older

Be bolder in your actions
And let them portray what you've been
Manifesting in your mind

Find peace in every day
In whatever way
Feels easy and delightful

Let the beauty of others
Radiate onto your skin
Until things feel better within

And when you are at your lowest
Know that you need not look further than yourself
To find comfort and strength.

Toast, Part 3

A different chapter
A different age
And Rebecca's put more poetry onto the page

Adrenaline highs are really what she seeks
In amongst her busy days,
Which she fills in ways
She didn't even know were possible
Without burning one's self out entirely.
And she does, sometimes —

She craves adventure and connection
With people, places and things:
She wants to feel every rush and sting life brings.

Her norm is not drinking with friends 'til the sun comes up
It never really was.
Instead, it's being tucked up in bed to read a new book
And she finds that she's hooked
In seconds.

But even on the days where she can't see past tomorrow,
Is feeling under the weather,
Wondering whether to give up...
Her Mum is there
With love and care
With a hug to give and not to borrow.

She picks her up in the way she always has,
With an embrace that heals
Feels complete
And of course
                with toast.

Be Still

Be still
My beating heart
Beating my mind
Pounding
Heart
Beat
Sharp
Intakes of breath
Don't fill my lungs enough for me to breathe properly
And I'm lingering in emptiness
Craving a whole piece of me
A small segment
Anything
Just a moment of serenity:
That'll be enough.

Like what you're doing is enough;
Enough,
You're doing enough
But enough to you is changing

There's more to enough than before
So it's no wonder your heart is racing —
You're out again before you've entered the door.

Poor mind
Being beaten, battered, bruised
Buzzing with stings
Even worker bees rest
They do
Even worker bees rest
So you
Should rest too.

Tequila Sunset

On the cusp of day
Turning to night,
The tequila sunset sits beautifully on the summer sky's face.

The light blue and pastel yellow,
Almost hazy in their blend
Embrace my gaze.

I feel nineteen again,
Inhale cocktails and wine like I'll be fine tomorrow
But tomorrow doesn't matter
Because I'm pounding the ground with my size 5 Nikes
As I jump and belt the iconic anthem that is Mr Brightside.

I never want this moment to end.
So let's pretend to be young forever.

I am suspended between the stars and tequila.

Sounds from the speaker rattle my bones
And I move in wild abandon.
Bodies bounce and coexist in this blissful abyss
Of 90s dance hits —

Is this what heaven feels like?

I watch the blue and yellow light fade into night
And with bright-white phone torches leading the way
Everybody begins to settle and leave
And all I can think to say
Is how complete I felt
Like I'd been dealt the best deck of cards and won the game.

I leave that night: renewed,
With two cuddly toys from the Hook-A-Duck stand
And beautiful memories to treasure.

The Songbird

The songbird has been sitting in sorrowful slumber
For a while, now.
It doesn't know how this came to be.
It isn't free to fly
Or tear through the open air
With beautiful abandon
Instead
It sits and ponders
A little longer than it's meant to,
Taught to,
Told to.

But here
Between hanging lights
               And lanterns
And beneath the highest ceilings of all
This songbird spreads its dusty wings
And sings
Softly
      To begin with
             Building to the greatest crescendo it can muster.

Maybe it was the change of scene
Maybe it was knowing it would be heard
Really heard

Or maybe it was an instinct
A distinct and familiar action
To match the rousing of a feeling
A memory

I am home.

This is what I know
And though I to-and-fro
Fret and despair
There is wonder in memory
The living, breathing muscle of it all.

Shard

Maybe
When we are found at some point in our lives,
We are simply a shard of glass
Sharp
Dangerous
Previously broken and kicked to the side for somebody else
To find —

It would be a perfect vision,
A poetic love story, to say
That somebody found you
And smoothed your edges
Cleaned off the dirt
The blood
The sticky liquor

But that's not quite how it happens

You are found, picked up and held
And you talk
And you talk
And you talk
About how you were broken

It gets worse before it gets better
As you surrender to the truth

You tell them not to touch
But they do
They hurt too
But they want to help
Genuinely
Sincerely

And then suddenly
Without conscious choice or decision
You feel more whole than you ever felt before

And if you could
You'd bottle this moment, this confidence and ease
In a bottle of your own to keep.

Not for consumption though, just a reminder.

*

Remind me
When I am weak
How I have reached the peak once before
And rode the slopes back down on the other side
Like the tide leaving the shore
There is more
There is more
There is more

                  to come.

Toast, Part 4

One day I hope to have children of my own
And maybe when they're grown
They too, will be obsessed with toast.

I'll teach them that happiness starts with the small things:
The things we may sometimes take for granted
But return to, often.

First,
Drinking water combats thirst.

That going out for a walk will clear your head
More than staying in bed will.

That people will continue to love you, no matter how you feel.

That hugs are the real deal.

That anything that makes you feel loved, comforted and whole
Is something to be grateful for.

And that soothing the rumbles of your hungry tummy
With small squares of toasted bread
Will have you contented
In just a few bites.

Like I did when I was a kid,
Like it seemed when I was a teen,
Plenty when I was over twenty
And always,
With Mum.

Acknowledgements

This book would not have been possible without the incredible Rebecca Kenny at Bent Key Publishing; a force to be reckoned with! Words will never sum up just how grateful I am for your continued support and encouragement. Your impact on my poetry journey has been colossal — thank you, from the bottom of my heart!

To my dear friend and exceptional poet, Paul Daly, who first introduced me to spoken word in a corner of Edinburgh back in 2017. I cannot thank you enough.

To Lauren Cresswell, thank you for giving me the kind-hearted nudge and encouragement I needed to share my work publicly.

To the formidable community of poets and wordsmiths I have met in Manchester; you have shaped me as a poet, helped me up when I've been down and cheered the loudest when I have felt most myself on stage. It is a privilege to perform alongside you and you are a constant source of inspiration.

To my best friend, Jas, the biggest cheerleader a girl could ask for. Throughout every endeavour I have embarked upon, you have believed in me. I am grateful for your friendship.

To my sister, Jess, thank you for being there consistently along this journey. You champion my work ethic and proactivity in a way nobody else does.

To Mum, the best human being on the planet! Thank you for being with me every step of the way and for teaching me that if I want something, I should work hard and go and get it. The belief you have in me propels me forward in so many ways and I will never take that for granted. I am proud to be a Phythian and even more proud to be your daughter. I love you very much.

To Adam: the person to whom I am connected by intricate intimacies. Thank you for everything you have given me throughout our relationship in the many different forms it has taken. Thank you for always saying yes to hearing new poems I've written and thank you for showing me love in its purest form. I will never tire of seeing your face light up when I read *Doughnuts*.

Finally, thank you to you, dear reader, for choosing to read my book. You have made this toast-obsessed Mancunian very, very happy! I hope that through reading this book, you find acceptance towards your own perfectly messy tendencies, relationships and life, like I have.

About the Author

Rebecca Phythian is an actor, singer, poet from Manchester and a graduate of The Liverpool Institute for Performing Arts.

Rebecca's poetry has featured in online events with Beatfreeks Poetry Jam and Open Collab, Bristol along with Blackburn's Festival of Making 2021 and BBC Radio Manchester on multiple occasions.

Along with regular performances across the North West of England, Rebecca's poetry has previously been published in *The Liminal Zine* Issue 3, the *Buzzin' Bards* 2021 Anthology, Bolton zine *Natter-logue* Issue 1 and is due to be published in the *Changeling* Annual for 2023.

Rebecca founded and now co-runs her own theatre company, Blue Balloon Theatre, with her best friend, Jas. The company provides a platform for actors, poets and creatives to develop and showcase their own work in a supportive environment. Their ethos is to **make it happen**!

About Bent Key

It started with a key.

Bent Key is named after the bent front-door key that Rebecca Kenny found in her pocket after arriving home from hospital following her car crash. It is a symbol — of change, new starts, risk, and taking a chance on the unknown.

Bent Key is a micropublisher with ethics. We do not charge for submissions, we do not charge to publish and we make space for writers who may struggle to access traditional publishing houses, specifically writers who are neuro-divergent or otherwise marginalised. We never ask anyone to write for free, and we like to champion authentic voices.

All of our beautiful covers are designed by our graphic designer Sam at SMASH Illustration, a graphic design company based in Southport, Merseyside.

Find us online:
bentkeypublishing.co.uk

Instagram & Facebook   @bentkeypublishing
Twitter   @bentkeypublish